Meditations on Thomas Cole's Paintings

Meditations on Thomas Cole's Paintings

Poems by

Martin Willitts Jr

Cover design by Shay Culligan

ISBN: 978-1-954353-24-4

Kelsay Books
502 South 1040 East, A-119
American Fork, Utah, 84003

Acknowledgments

"The Course of Empires" series was published as a mico-chapbook (Origami Poems Project, 2020)

"Distant View of Niagara Falls" appeared in the *Aurorean* magazine

"Meditations on Thomas Cole's Clouds" series was published as a micro chapbook (Origami Poems Project, 2019)

I want to thank Heather Paroubek at the *Thomas Cole National Historic Site* for the generous use for the cover of "Peace at Sunset (Evening in the White Mountains)" (1827)

Contents

"…to look is one thing
to see is another"
—Margaret Gibson, *Reflection, Looking Straight Ahead*

I. Introduction

Thomas Cole was an American painter of the Hudson School (1801–1848). He lived most of his life in the village, Catskill, New York. He used the Chiaroscuro technique to represent light and shadow on three-dimensional objects. Many of his series are allegorical. He was also a poet. During the time period of these paintings was the "Monroe Doctrine" (1823), the "Erie Canal" was completed (1825), "Andrew Jackson Presidency" (1829–16), "Oregon Trail" (1830's), John Quincy Adams argues the "Armistad case" (1841). He saw the danger of expansion.

A visit to his art studio in Catskill, New York puts a traveler near many of the sites for his paintings.

Sunny Morning on the Hudson River

(1827)

this is the only morning we will ever know

fog breaking off a mountain as raindrifts
slow tempo arriving at the end

follow the trail of small rocks
along a hesitant river
a gust shivers the pine needles
light spirals
from a temporary cloud cover

small moments seem to last forever

this day will never last
and tomorrow will be different

as you enter this song of many days
this sheet music of moments
rifts in casual wind
this day curls with an orange-red sunrise
light reflecting off the stones
by the vibrating river
into the pines

View on Lake Winnipiseogee

(1828)

1.

all days start this way
slowly and assuredly
small blessings
easing into the world without fanfare

someone is learning what it is like
to be alive within these moments
within those aspects of love
about how everything is better

the world has such broad strokes
we see only last a very short time
whatever we see becomes perceptible
all days should be this way

2.

among the chestnuts
and hard green crab apples
the inevitable is waiting

a brown and pale grey waxwing
with dripped red sealing wax wingtips
forages in the woods

tumultuous cold winds waver
a ripple of yellow wildflowers
a song entering the body

these blessings
give song we did not have
to shape love within us

II. The Course of Empires

This is a progressive series of five paintings created by
Thomas Cole,1833–1836

The Course of Empire

Sometimes, I am afraid the empire will lead to decay
and gluttony. The way we ravage forests
to make life for small villages
is greed for greed's sake: do we need to take away
one for the purpose of the other?

Oaks fall for the course of the empire,
making way for small, immaculate white churches
with fingers of bell towers
never ringing for mercy.

A few humble settlements grow
to edge away the pines and white spruce.
The pumpkin patches surrender to the store front
where flour is sold by white bagsful.
All this has happened slowly over time,
until next, a center green gazebo
is surrounded by other stores,
where wagons hitch long enough
to take in the view. Building accelerates
with excitement as the maples fall.

And, what, if anything,
does the large boulder
overlooking the progress of the valley
think of the swelling kingdom below?

Perhaps, it will have its say, someday.

1. The Savage State

Eden must have looked like this—
untamed by limitless trees, a dim light
filtering through the leaves with auras.
Adam had not appeared yet.

The forest was humming with small animals,
peepers and cicadas, wrens and cardinals.
An eagle perched on a boulder,
readying to unfurl into the infused light.

Adam was not there to witness,
to name everything he saw.
What was here was not meant for his eyes.
The world did not need him at this time.

Dawn was storming. It knew
Adam would arrive and ruin it all,
wrecking the landscape and peace,
not resting until it is civilized at last.

Through the wilderness of dismal light,
Adam came paddling upstream,
noticing all the woods he had to clear-cut
to make way for barns and factories.

Adam was a surveyor measuring boundaries.
Small changes were escalating into bigger ones.

2. The Arcadian or Pastoral State

                    Do not be deceived
by the pastoral, idyllic fields
sky clearing for a spring morning;

          trouble is hiding in that calmness,
an undercurrent of impending danger
no one can see.

                         Up river,
using the forked peak of a boulder
as a guide,

               someone is chopping trees,
someone plows land into submission.
Notice the trimmed, organized lawns.

          This is not God's plan.
People are building a boat. Someone herds
God's sheep into the fulcrum of the fields.

          What Greek God is worshipped?
At the megalithic white columned temple,
sacrificial pale smoke curls out.

                    And, look,
that boat is a warship. A child idolizing a soldier
prepares for his first war. What God is this?

3. The Consummation of Empire

A summer day shines
off the colonnaded marble buildings
resembling the best architecture of Rome.

We have built this
to last a thousand centuries, a testament
to our control over the land.

Boats with lateen sails
take this news throughout the world.

Our scarlet-robed leader
is strutting like a male cardinal
over the promenade
between two marble towers
lighting the way to the future.

4. Destruction

A boat is sailing away from the tempest
as the enemy destroys the city.

                        Isn't this
the way of all empires—someone else
destroys them?

                    Tidal waves rise
and fall; empires ebb. Smoke obliterates
skies, darkens all progress.
                                And for what?

                The enemy is at the gate.
Survivors are fleeing the erasure of the city
like Troy.
The city is sacked, buildings are plundered,
women are raped. Any progress is undone.

All triumphs are being destroyed, turned
to ash, gutted,
columns tore to the ground.
                            The bridge is gone,
and a makeshift one sags
under the weight of conquest.

They have beheaded our statue to a hero
whose name escapes me. The dead fall
wherever they were
                killed in the straining light,
in the affluence of death.

5. Desolation

This is the finale of all
powerful civilizations, this afterwards
when they collapse.
The world returns to primal state,
reclaiming what was taken away.

Remnants of former buildings lose out to nature.
Ivy covers them.
Broken light towers no longer search for visitors.
The ruins of the bridge are unsafe to cross.
A single column is used for nesting birds.
None of nature mourns for humanity.

The moon has risen over the ruined river.
The day reaches its crescendo,
glistening on one standing pillar.

III. Meditations on Thomas Cole's *Clouds*

"The south wind blew strongly, and dark masses of cloud moved across the twilight sky, the heralds of approaching storm. A leaden hue overspread the vale, the woods, and the distant mountains. How contagious is gloom! A flow of melancholy thoughts and feelings overwhelmed me for a time. I thought of the uncertainty of life, its bootless toil, and brevity. The south wind, I thought, would still continue to blow, and bring up its dark clouds for ages after my works, and all the reputation I might gain had faded away, and become as though they had never been—swept by the wing of time into oblivion's gulf. And shall it be? Shall the spirit, that mysterious principle, unknown even to itself, that vivifies this earth, and generates these thoughts, sink also into the gloomy gulf of nonexistence, nor feel again created Beauty, nor see the Nature that it loved so much? It cannot be. The Great Originator, the Mighty One, the Unspeakable, hath not created for purposes vain and useless this power of conceiving…"

Thomas Cole, A journal entry for May 31, 1835

Clouds

(1838)

1.

whenever I feel superior
God impresses me
with such awe
my mouth cannot speak

all I can do
is paint with my heart
the wordlessness
changing within me
as frequently as clouds

2.

whatever is in darkness
will surrender to Light

whatever is mysterious
will be revealed
to us some day

whatever saddens us
will be lifted
like clouds
from our eyes

what we hear
will be the unspoken
if we listen
within the silence

3.

whatever is lifted
out of the silence
has another hidden message
we need to decipher

the image is cloudy
unless we have patience
to discern

it shifts like clouds
we must be quick
to catch a glimpse
before it breaks apart

4.

we need to understand
we are loved

we may feel lonely
abandoned
forgotten

we are remembered

remember when we looked at clouds
naming their shapes
as they transformed

we are like that
changing all of the time

we may never see the change
happening
and we cannot prevent it

     5.

all the reputation I might gain
that could fade away
is not something worth worrying us
during the Presence of God

we cannot worry about
the uncertainty of life
for it will form and fade
as often as clouds

this power of conceiving
within love
is within all of us
willing to be open
to receiving

     6.

all things are possible
if we believe

small miracles inside us
a kind of resurrection

clouds smear with light
entering us

we are never the same
nor is a millennium of fallen rain

nor baby hawks opening yellow beaks
trusting their emptiness will be filled

IV. The Voyage of Life series

(1842)

This series reflects all four seasons as well as the passage of four periods of a person's life.

The Voyage of Life: Childhood

Water falls silent only for you.
Leaves shush in dawn-light
so that you might find the ever-making fields.

Waterlilies rise from their hidden depths
to try to claim this love of light.
Anyone searching for light will find it.

A horse races after the light
on the curving land
of the Creator's palm.

Light finds you
and saturates you. It finds you
all the way from the other side of the world.

The Voyage of Life: Youth

I laid on the grass and asked
when the deer came by last

the distant barking gunfire
echoing their death threats
and I shriveled like being struck too often

geese had left their scat nearby
before snatching the sky
in their webbed feet

the grass recalled when I was boy
spreading out angel wings
my shadow flew into the quiet

the grass knew I was introspective
and dreamy
and thankfully I've never changed

The Voyage of Life: Manhood

I'm searching for anyone I might recognize
in the light still skimming the horizon
during this late autumn hours

the sky narrows its blue tempera paint
over the rapids
falling among the weight of shadows

I can't see far enough ahead
to know what will happen
or why the horizon darkens like ravens

in the blue and awful dark
someone is calling my name
either warning or inviting

The Voyage of Life: Old Age

Sailing into the winter,
leading into deep darkness
I've allowed the journey to take me
to a place I've never been.

When I fought against the current,
the distance took me far
from where I wanted to be
to where I've never been.

I thought I controlled the till,
turning towards the wind, but
I never controlled anything;
My battered ship went where it would.

The waves are old and tired.
The journey ends straight on.
The more I learned, the less I knew.
Yet more was still ahead.

Dark water is all I can see,
then angels descending—
or is it light,
or is it Spirit guiding me?

V. Other Paintings

View from Mount Holyoke, Northampton, Massachusetts, after a Thunderstorm

(commonly known as The Oxbow)

(1836)

The dark has a wilderness all its own.
A thunderstorm splintered trees on the cliff.

Rain ebbs, wandering away
dreamingly, stroked by light

through films of misty rain. Calm hovers,
birds proclaiming, suggesting change.

Peace approaches: the worse is over.
The storm ceases over the Connecticut River.

Cultivated lands, engineered by hands,
have logging blemishes with damp

and muddy trails. Thomas Cole is painting,
as he contemplates the passing rain.

Lake with Dead Trees

(1825)

In snag trees, light finds
skeleton trees
removed of leaves, bark,

branches, broken away.
The tree tried to avoid the storm
that humbled them into surrender,

exposed to the elements,
chewed raw, sun-wrecked
with shades of frail yellow.

They are surrounded by signs of life:
flourishing trees, emerging,
renewing, mirrored in the lake.

Some trees had fallen.
Their decay will enrich the soil.
Mushrooms will claim those trees.

The Catskills ignore time; loss
is replaced. Light shifts, decreasing
and renewing time.

A View of the Two Lakes and Mountain House, Catskill Mountains, Morning

(1848)

light by itself has no color
but the jay does
singing unspeakable love

each day
he is constantly reviving
from the unspoken to the spoken

all eventually enter the unknown

light moves slowly
holding its breath
afraid of breaking this hushed world

all fear the slightest disturbance
will ruin the mystery of extreme silence

Distant View of Niagara Falls

(1830)

scrimshaw clouds write this day into our hearts
singing over the distance
from whale bones

out of the sky's cupboard floats a buttery sun
working out what the day tries to say
in a distant hum of falls

embellishments from the peepers
disturb the air
with their sweetheart music

this world of noise disappears into the background
all afterthoughts
bending closer and closer to notice

Kaaterskill Falls

(1826)

this two-tier waterfall rushes you into dreams
cascading down sandstone ledges

scarlet autumnal leaves in channels of light
from the anvil of looming clouds

time condenses from spiraling water
although nothing moving ever remains

where we are going does not matter
it is the arrival that does

Clove from Haines Falls

(1827)

The dark-green hemlock forest in fall
knows the end of the summer is near:
ablaze by rust tints and ruddy leaves

in the worrisome loss of light
narrowing in the ravine. It is time
to move on, shadows rubbing against

rock ledges or gnarled hands of dead trees.
Seasons change and light fades,
a moment's visit never stays.

Expulsion from the Garden of Eden

(1827–28)

It wasn't the apple that caused the expulsion,
it wasn't listening to the early warning signs.
It wasn't the black and yellow snake they blamed;
it was the effects of their bad decisions.
They needed an exit, so they made one up.

From the Top of Kaaterskill Falls

(1826)

Light is trapped in the waterfall's undertow,
trembling with leaves in the breeze at dusk.
The land is resting quietly.

Water collects blue violet colors,
stirring yellow sun-ripples.
A sparrow offers invocation to the light.

Geese swish, swish, swish departure,
elongating our sadness behind them.
The year turns another season.

A cabin on the lake anticipates
sunset's garnet reflection. A loon warbles
trembling desperation across the water

like violets in a whispered, chilled wind.
A sparrow takes music from branch to branch
where water rushes over a cliff.

Geese shush away like clouds.
Tip-toe caution waits.
We are chosen to find surprises.

Travel to where the river bends.
Arrival depends on *otherwise* airstreams.
Life always carries us at its own pace.

Landscape, the Seat of Mr. Featherstonhaugh in the Distance

(1826)

Border Leicester sheep graze like clouds
can never keep in line

the wavering whip-poor-will regrets
the season about to end
taking its promise
of lasting

the peeks of light shows
impending storm reflection
on the languid water

the immobile sheep
dwell in the secret of nature
wait
like breaths of stratus clouds

their mouths ticking with grass

a woodpecker raps incessantly on a dead tree
its staccato message

Peace at Sunset (Evening in the White Mountains)

(1827)

when the land was unexplored
no one had laid an ax to a tree

nightfall stormed over the mountains
then a hawk's final cry

there was peace in the valley
there was serenity in the stillness

this was before the wilderness-taming
before the silence was clean-cut progress

the world was as temporary as mist
swooping from the white mountain

The Pilgrim of the Cross at the End of His Journey

(1846)

We never live so long we can't learn love.
We never know so much
we can't ignore the light in pattering rain.

Some of us never live long enough
to realize what we have done
and how it affects others.

When all our words fail to be heard,
rain will collapse as retribution.
We need to learn to forgive.

VI. Meditation: The Silent Energy of Nature: *View on the Schoharie*

"It was not that the jagged precipices were lofty, that the encircling woods were the dimmest shade, or that the waters were profoundly deep; but that over all, rocks, wood, and water, brooded the spirit of repose, and the silent energy of nature stirred the soul to its innermost depths."

—Thomas Cole

View on the Schoharie

(1826)

1.

in the blossoming periwinkle sky
seashell clouds are the longest part of language
we hold back our words

a waterfall kneels at its base
where it spends time
before moving on

a wren flies inside the looseness
where all living moments hold their breath
the lavender night fills God's canvas

2.

when entering a forest
do not be surprised
if our souls want to remain

after our senses are overwhelmed
it takes time to settle down
every image coming into focus

we can't stop noticing
message scribbling in our heart
there's no sidestepping how we feel

About the Author

Martin Willitts Jr is a retired Librarian living in Syracuse, New York. He was nominated for 17 Pushcart and 15 Best of the Net awards. Winner of the *2012 Big River Poetry Review's William K. Hathaway Award; 2013 Bill Holm Witness Poetry Contest; 2013 "Trees" Poetry Contest; 2014 Broadsided award; 2014 Dylan Thomas International Poetry Contest; Rattle Ekphrastic Challenge, June 2015, Editor's Choice; Rattle Ekphrastic Challenge, Artist's Choice, November 2016, Stephen A. DiBiase Poetry Prize, 2018.* He won *a Central New York Individual Artist Award* and provided "Poetry on The Bus" which had 48 poems in local buses including 20 bi-lingual poems from 7 different languages.

His 24 chapbooks include "Falling In and Out of Love" (Pudding House Publications, 2005), "Lowering Nets of Light" (Pudding House Publications, 2007), "The Garden of French Horns" (Pudding House Publications, 2008), "Baskets of Tomorrow" (Flutter Press, 2009), "The Girl Who Sang Forth Horses" (Pudding House Publications, 2010), "Van Gogh's Sunflowers for Cezanne" (Finishing Line Press, 2010), "Why Women Are A Ribbon Around A Bomb" (Last Automat, 2011), "Protest, Petition, Write, Speak: Matilda Joslyn Gage Poems" (Matilda Joslyn Gage Foundation, 2011), "Secrets No One Wants To Talk About" (Dos Madres Press, 2011), "How to Find Peace" (Kattywompus Press, 2012), "Playing The Pauses In The Absence Of Stars" (Main Street Rag, 2012), "No Special Favors" (Green Fuse Press, 2012), "The Constellations of Memory and Forgiveness" (Seven Circles Press, web book, 2014), "A Is For Aorta" (Kind of Hurricane Press, e-book, 2014), *National Chapbook Contest* winning "William Blake, Not Blessed Angel But Restless Man" (Red Ochre Press, 2014), "Swimming in the Ladle of Stars" (Kattywompus Press,2014),"City Of Tents" (Crisis Chronicles Press, 2014), "The Way Things Used To Be" (Writing Knights Press, 2014), "Late All Night Sessions with Charlie "the Bird" Parker and the Members of

Birdland, in Take-Three" (A Kind Of a Hurricane Press, 2015), "The Burnt-Over District" (e-book, Icarus Books, 2015), "Martin Willitts Jr Greatest Hits" (Kattywompus Press, 2016), *Turtle Island Editor's Choice Award* for his chapbook, "The Wire Fence Holding Back the World" (Flowstone Press, 2016), "Nasturtiums in Snow Understand Green Is Coming" (Foothills Press, 2018), "You Enter, and it All Falls Apart" (Flutter Press, 2019).

His 17 full-length books include "The Secret Language of the Universe" (March Street Press, 2006), "The Hummingbird" (March Street Press, 2009), "The Heart Knows, Simply, What It Needs: Poems based on Emily Dickinson, her life and poetry" (Aldrich Press, 2012), "Art is an Impression of What an Artist Sees" (Edgar and Lenore Publishing House, 2013), *National Ecological Award* winner for "Searching for What You Cannot See" (Hiraeth Press, 2013), "Before Anything, There Was Mystery" (Flutter Press, 2014), "Irises, the Lightning Conductor For Van Gogh's Illness" (Aldrich Press, 2014), "God Is Not Amused with What You Are Doing in Her Name" (Aldrich Press, 2015), "How to Be Silent" (FutureCycle Press, 2016), "Dylan Thomas and the Writer's Shed" (FutureCycle Press, 2017), "Three Ages of Women" (Deerbrook Editions, 2017), "The Uncertain Lover" (Dos Madres Press, 2018), "News from the Slow Country" (Aldrich Press, 2019), "Home Coming Celebration" (FutureCycle Press, 2019), the *2019 Blue Light Award* winner "The Temporary World", "Unexpected" (Duck Lake Books, 2020), and "Unfolding of Love" (Wipf and Stock Publishers, 2020.)

He is an editor for Comstock Review.

www.ingramcontent.com/pod-product-compliance
Lightning Source LLC
Chambersburg PA
CBHW071358090426
42738CB00012B/3161